WHY YOU LOOK LIKE YOU *WHEREAS* I TEND TO LOOK LIKE ME

WHY YOU LOOK LIKE YOU WHEREAS I TEND TO LOOK LIKE ME

By Charlotte Pomerantz

**PICTURES BY ROSEMARY WELLS
AND SUSAN JEFFERS**

YOUNG SCOTT BOOKS

For Dan and Sally

Photograph on page 58 from Culver Pictures, Inc.

CONTENTS

Mendel the modest monk
Planted the garden pea
To find out why you look like you
Whereas I tend to look more like me.

People, of course, had always said,
As they peered into the baby's bed:
"He looks like his father, but not like his mother.
He has the same nose as his grandfather's brother."

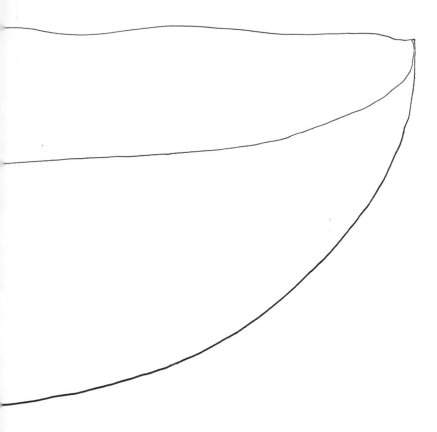

Farmers for centuries knew this was true
Of animals, fruits, and the crops they grew.
And so, for example, they carefully bred
A short-legged dog to crawl under a shed . . .

And chase away foxes and weasels and moles,
And follow quick rabbits down rabbity holes.

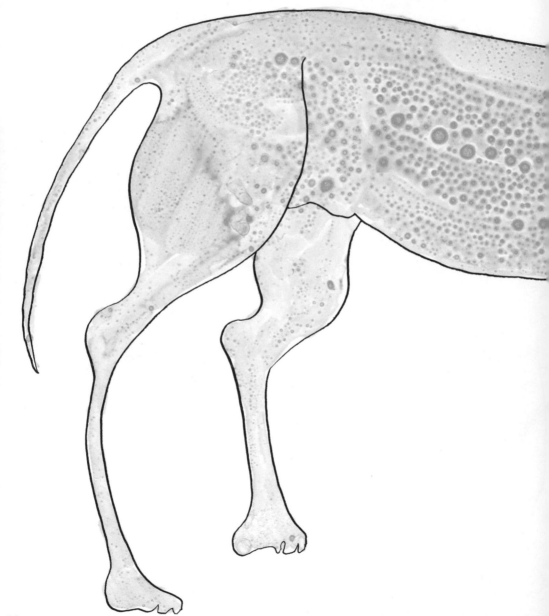

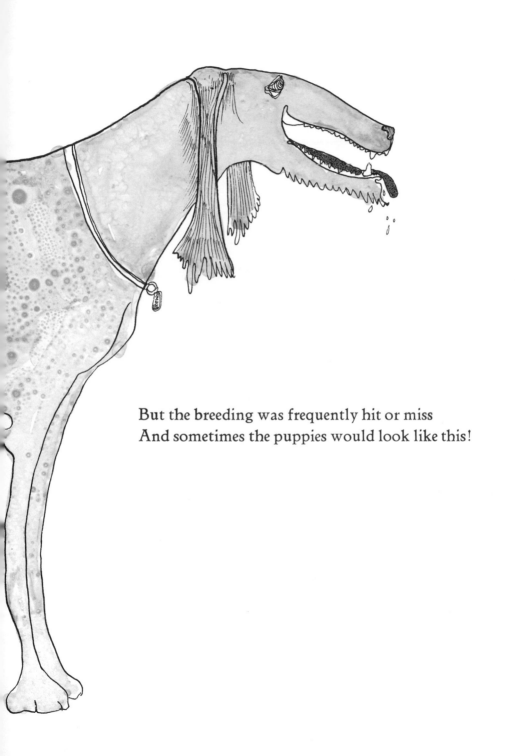

But the breeding was frequently hit or miss
And sometimes the puppies would look like this!

Some scientists, working with plants as their tools,
Tried to discover some definite rules.
But plants, just like people, had so many traits,
So many sizes, shapes, colors, and weights,
That scientists, piling up notes in great stacks,
Were utterly baffled by so many facts!

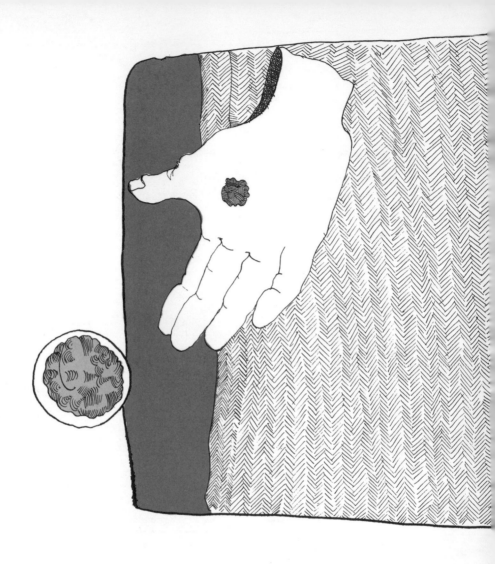

But Mendel the monk thought, "I know what I'll do.
I'll choose opposite traits and follow them through.
Methinks I will study the garden pea,
To look for the *whys* of heredity.

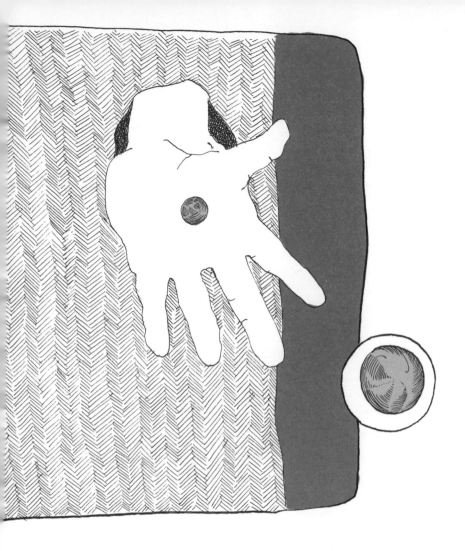

I'll choose size of plant *or* I'll choose shape of seed,
But for only *one thing* at a time will I breed."

So he put two pea seeds in the ground—
One was wrinkled and one was round.

And when they had offspring, guess what he found?
Guess if their offspring were wrinkled or round?

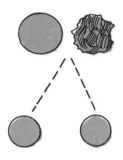

Did you guess half were wrinkled and half were round?
That's *one* wrong guess, 'cause here's what he found:
Every one of their offspring was round!

So he put the offspring into the ground . . .
Every one, as we know, was round.
And when *they* sprouted, guess what he found?
Did you guess that *all* of their offspring were round?

That's *two* wrong guesses, 'cause here's what he found:
One was wrinkled and *three* were round!

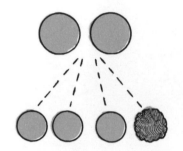

But what, you ask, does the lowly pea
Have to do with you and me?

Well . . .
Mendel wondered if every trait
Comes to peas and children straight
From one parent or the other . . .
Which is why both you and I
Look just like our father and mother . . .

Unless, of course, they're very small
And you are over six feet tall!

And both of them have tiny feet . . .
While yours reach halfway down the street!

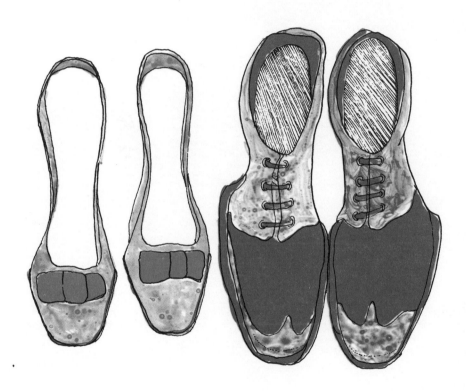

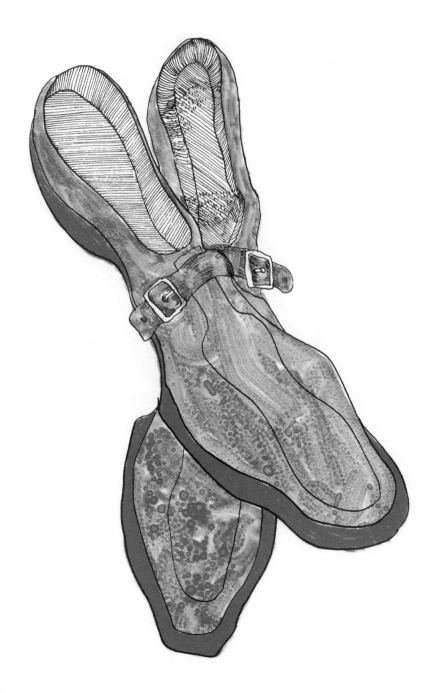

Mendel was puzzled by problems like these—
So he studied the traits of ten thousand peas.

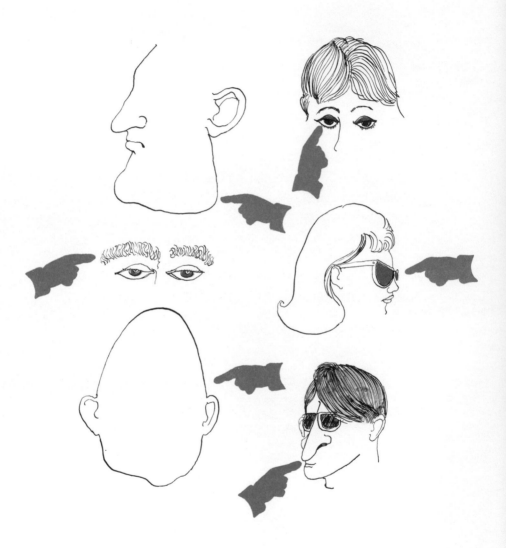

Wrinkled and round are two traits of a pea.
Thousands of traits make up you and me.

Today we know what a trait really means.
It's a characteristic made up of some genes.

A gene is a tiny part of a cell,
And a cell is the start of you and me . . .

Millions of genes inside of our cells
Help shape our looks and what we will be.

One bundle of genes comes down from your ma.
The other you get by way of your pa.
All of which means
You're the mix of their genes.

Some genes are "bold";
Some genes are "shy."
One shows right away;
One shows by-and-by.

Every trait has at least two genes,
which combine in at least four ways.
The genes may be dominant-dominant,
which results in a dominant trait,

Or recessive-recessive,
which results in a recessive trait,

Or dominant-recessive,
which results in a dominant trait,

Or recessive-dominant,
which results in a dominant trait.

A shy gene is called a recessive gene;
For, like wrinkledness, it is *not* always seen.
A bold gene is called a dominant gene;
For, like roundness in peas, it *always* is seen.

If, of two genes, one is dominant,
That trait will be the most prominent.
For example, in human beings:
The curly gene always will dominate
Over the gene for hair that is straight.

So, if your momma has curly hair,
At least one dominant gene is there.
If poppa's hair is straight, that means
Poppa has two recessive genes.
For if one dominant gene were there,
Poppa, of course, would have curly hair.

Though your folks have two genes for a trait,
They each pass but one gene to you . . .
Which means for that given trait,
You don't get four genes—you get *two*.

Some examples:
If mom has two genes for curly
And pop has two genes for straight
That means you'll inherit a gene of each kind
But the curly will dominate.

Or:
If mom has one gene for curly
And one gene for hair that is straight,
And pop has two straight-haired genes,
What is *your* inherited fate?
You may get the straight gene from mom,
And another straight gene from your pop.
In which case, though mom has curly hair,
You will have straight hair on the top.

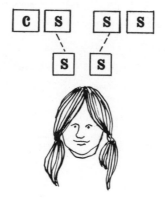

However, it's only fair to say
That it might happen the opposite way.
You might inherit ma's curly gene
And the straight-haired gene from your pop.
In which case, despite your poppa's straight hair
You'll inherit your momma's mop.

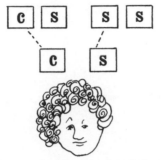

But suppose mom and pop *both* have curly hair,
And yours is as straight as a stick.
You may well think, "It's most unfair
Of nature to play such a trick."

Not so, for each had a gene for straight hair,
And you got one from mom, one from pop.
And once inside you, they made a pair,
Which accounts for the funny flip-flop!

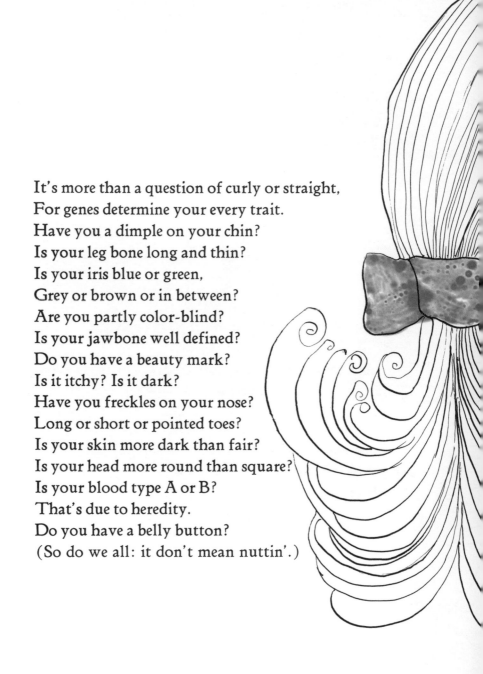

It's more than a question of curly or straight,
For genes determine your every trait.
Have you a dimple on your chin?
Is your leg bone long and thin?
Is your iris blue or green,
Grey or brown or in between?
Are you partly color-blind?
Is your jawbone well defined?
Do you have a beauty mark?
Is it itchy? Is it dark?
Have you freckles on your nose?
Long or short or pointed toes?
Is your skin more dark than fair?
Is your head more round than square?
Is your blood type A or B?
That's due to heredity.
Do you have a belly button?
(So do we all: it don't mean nuttin'.)

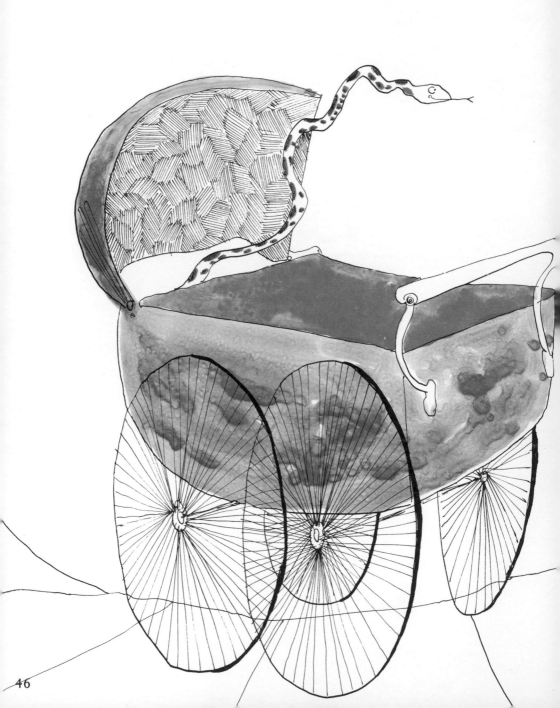

Are you a boy . . . a girl . . . or a snake?
If you're a snake, there's been some mistake!

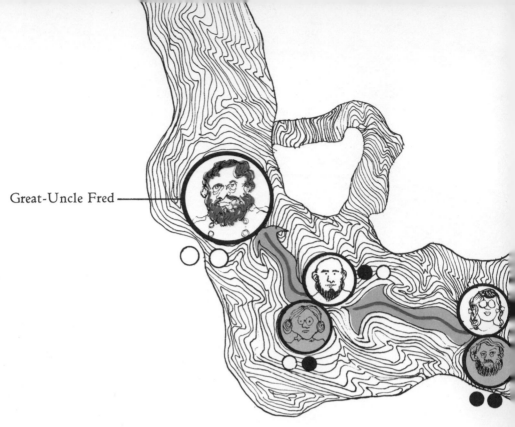

Great-Uncle Fred

To sum up:

A shy gene may skip a whole generation—
Then meet up with its mate in a distant relation.

Such was the case of my Great-Uncle Fred
When two shy genes met inside him and said:
"Freddy, old chap, like we always say, better late than never—
For now we two recessive genes can dominate you forever!"

For Freddy, you see, had a flaming *red* beard
In a family where only black beards appeared—
Which seemed rather odd, if not downright weird.

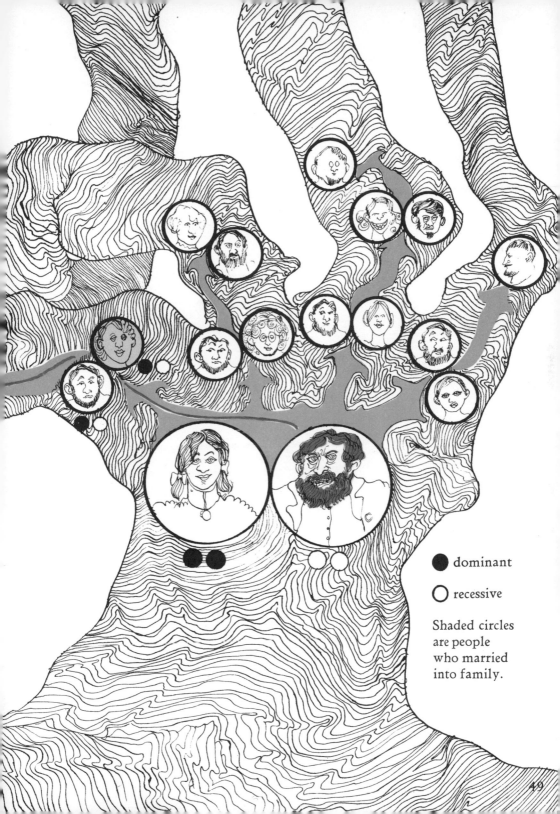

dominant

recessive

Shaded circles
are people
who married
into family.

49

All of which means, though I know it sounds silly,
You may strongly resemble your dear old Aunt Tilly.

Or even your grandfather's Great-Uncle Billy!

UNCLE BILLY

51

Such are the laws of heredity
Which govern you, me, and the garden pea.

If you want to find out
how Mendel crossed one
pea plant with another...
turn the page and
follow the details

A Pea Plant

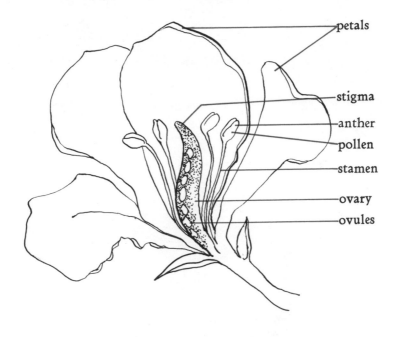

petals

stigma

anther

pollen

stamen

ovary

ovules

Some Details of the Flower
of the Pea Plant

The ovary contains ovules from which new plants grow, but only if they are fertilized by the pollen.

The pollen is in a sac (the anther) on top of the stamens.

When the pollen lands on the stigma, the first step of fertilization begins.

What Happens In Nature:

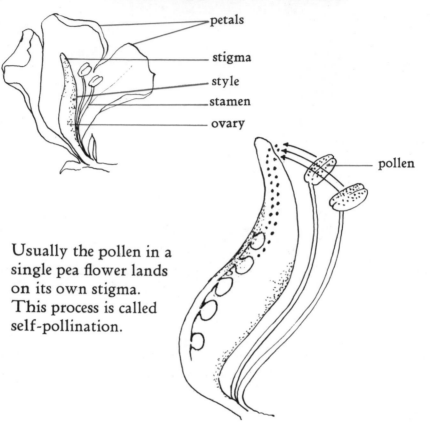

petals

stigma

style

stamen

ovary

pollen

Usually the pollen in a
single pea flower lands
on its own stigma.
This process is called
self-pollination.

Each pollen grain grows into a pollen tube, which pushes
its way down through the style to the ovary. Here the con-
tents of the pollen tube join with the content of the ovule.
In this way the ovules become fertilized.
Then they become seeds.

What Mendel Did:

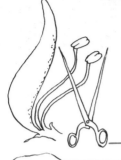

He cut off the stamens on a flower, so their pollen could not fertilize the stigma of the same flower.

scissors

bag

Then he put a bag on the stigma, so that pollen from other flowers could not get to the stigma.

brush

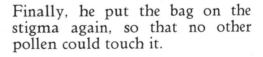

Then he took pollen from another plant (which he knew to be a pure strain) and brushed it onto the stigma.

Finally, he put the bag on the stigma again, so that no other pollen could touch it.

In this way, Mendel knew exactly which strains he was crossing. Thus, he could follow the chain of heredity.

GREGOR MENDEL

Gregor Mendel

(1822-1884)

A little more than a hundred years ago, a plump, blue-eyed little monk named Gregor Mendel stood before a local gathering of some forty scientists and read a paper about his experiments with the garden pea—the kind that we eat.

The year was 1865. The town was Brünn, Austria (now Czechoslovakia). The place was the Modern School. The occasion was a meeting of the Brünn Society for the Study of Natural Science. Among the scientists present were an astronomer, a geologist, a chemist, and several botanists. These scientists regarded Mendel with fondness and respect. Nevertheless, the minutes of the meeting show that no questions were asked and no discussion took place.

Why was it that able scientists failed to recognize the significance of Mendel's discoveries? (Even today, were you to go to the library and look up Mendel's historic paper, *Experiments in Plant Hybridization,* published in 1866, you would probably find it as dry as a wrinkled pea—recessive.) Too much was said, too fast, and too abstractly. But the basic reason was that Mendel was wildly original. The idea of putting together statistics, algebra, and gardening was unconventional and baffling.

Indeed, Mendel was *not* a conventional man. He combined in his work a profound love of gardening with a rare ability to ask the right questions.

Mendel's interest in plants and animal life began in early childhood, when he lived and worked on his father's farm and orchard in Heinzendorf, near Brünn. There he learned about crossing (hybridization) in trees and flowers for fruit-growing, and bee-keeping—subjects also taught in his village schools.

Mendel was an excellent student. Unfortunately, his parents could not support him through high school and he had to scratch for a living, suffering continual hunger as he pored over his books.

He decided to enter the monastery at Brünn and to become a priest. This was due to his being extremely poor as well as religious. He knew, too, that the monastery was a leading center of scientific activity. Best of all, it had a fine botanical garden.

At the monastery, Mendel was often visited by the schoolboys whom he taught in the local high school—as a substitute teacher. (He was never able to get a permanent teaching license because of the rigid and conventional system of government examinations in Austria at that time.) His pupils were always sure of a warm reception and a chance to see Mendel's tame fox, birds, mice, and other pets, as well as his experimental garden.

In this garden, Mendel had been growing pea plants for eight years. By the time he stood up to read his paper, he had planted ten thousand of them!

Beginning with pure seeds, he cross-pollinated the parent plants by the methods shown on pages 56-57. He then harvested the offspring, counted them, sorted them, and kept records of each *separate* trait. Others had kept records before, but they had viewed the plant *as a whole* and were confused by its complexities. In all, Mendel kept records of seven distinct traits of peas, which he grew in the same garden under the same conditions.

From his observations, he reached the conclusions presented in this book. His terminology was somewhat different from ours. What we call "genes," he called "elements." What we call "traits," he called "characters."

We now believe that all forms of life (organisms) begin with a single cell. At about the time of Mendel's death, scientists were able to study the cell directly, by staining it with a dye and examining it under a microscope. Except in single-cell organisms, the first cell grows by dividing into two cells, which divide into four, and so on, until there are millions and billions of cells in the organism. (A human baby at birth has 200,000,000,000 —two hundred billion—cells.) The original cell, and all cells that come from it, contains a core, called a *nucleus*. Within each nucleus are tiny rodlike structures called *chromosomes*. Every plant and animal has a given number of chromosomes. The garden pea has 14 (7 pairs); a mouse has 40 (20 pairs); man has 46 (23 pairs).

Chromosomes, which differ in size and shape, are made up of hundreds or thousands of tiny entities called *genes*. Since the chromosomes are paired, the genes are paired. The word *gene* comes from the Greek word meaning "to give birth to," and the science of heredity is now called *genetics*. Its students are called *geneticists*.

At first, geneticists thought that what Mendel called a dominant or recessive "element" was really an independent gene. But the picture is more complicated. Although thousands of traits are determined by a single

gene from each parent (such as straight and curly hair),
thousands of other traits are determined by more than
two genes.

But all this enormously complex knowledge was far
in the future when Mendel presented his paper to his
baffled fellow scientists. The statistical account of his
endless experiments was tedious and difficult to follow.
Further, Mendel's "elements" were not tangible or prov-
able directly: they were inferences, almost guesses. He
was, in effect, asking men of science to take something
on faith.

The truth is that Mendel was way ahead of his time.
No one quite saw the point of mixing algebra and peas.
Certainly no one knew he was present at the birth of
a new science: the science of genetics.

Although Mendel's paper was sent to more than one
hundred libraries, scientific societies, and universities
throughout Europe, it lay forgotten for some thirty
years. Then, in 1900, sixteen years after Mendel's
death, three scientists, working independently in three
different countries, discovered the paper and recognized
its value.

Mendel's judgment was vindicated. "My time will
come," he had once said to a friend.

Mendel's paper on the garden pea was the high point
of his scientific life. In 1868 he was elected abbot, that is,
the head of the monastery. The garden now available to
him was much larger than the narrow strip on which he
had grown his peas, but he soon found that his duties
as abbot took up most of his time and energy. Still, he
never completely ceased to grow and crossbreed his
beloved flowers and fruit trees, and even found time
to organize the local fire brigade.

Mendel's sense of the wonder of science and man's mind developed early in life. Here is part of a long poem he wrote as a teenager:

> . . . Unceasing toil,
> The ennoblement and development of his energies,
> These are man's lot here below.
> But unfading are the laurels of him . . .
> Who with the full light of understanding
> Seeks and finds the mysterious depths of knowledge,
> . . . [to] dispel
> The gloomy power of superstition
> Which now oppresses the world.

Mendel died in 1884. A large number of friends and admirers attended his funeral. They included scientists, teachers, Catholic clergymen, the Protestant pastor, and the Jewish rabbi. There were also members of the Heinzendorf fire brigade and a great many of the poor people of Brünn, who knew and loved the kindly and modest monk.

Not one suspected that the father of modern genetics had passed away.

About the Author

CHARLOTTE POMERANTZ' two previous books for William R. Scott both reflect a point of view that is refreshing and provocative. *The Moon Pony* ". . . is about a Negro child's dream of a ride to the moon on a white pony. It preserves the delicate balance between the real world and the imaginary." (*Time*, Dec. 1, 1967). *Ask The Windy Sea* recounts a young boy's amble along the beach looking for a lost caterpillar, garnering information and ideas from people he meets along the way.

A graduate of Sarah Lawrence College, Miss Pomerantz has worked as a saleslady, researcher, editor, and writer. She and her husband, Carl Marzani, live in New York City with their young daughter, Gabrielle Rose.

About the Artists

ROSEMARY WELLS and SUSAN JEFFERS are respectively Chairman of the Board and President of a small graphic design studio in New York City.

Mrs. Wells, a painter and printmaker, studied at the Museum School in Boston. Her imaginative illustrations of a number of books, among them *The Duke of Plaza Toro, Hungry Fred, A Song to Sing O,* and *John and the Rarey,* have received wide critical acclaim. She lives in New York City with her husband.

Miss Jeffers, a well-known graphic designer, has designed jackets for many books. She is a graduate of Pratt Institute and lives in Brooklyn.